The Ultimate Salmon Cookbook

By CARLA HUTSON

Table of Contents

Grilled Citrus Salmon

Prepare to be transported to a tropical paradise with our Grilled Citrus Salmon. This menu combines the juiciness of salmon with the bright, zesty notes of citrus, creating a perfect harmony on your palate. The marinade, featuring a blend of fresh orange and lemon juices, garlic, and a hint of cilantro, imparts a refreshing burst of flavors. Grilling the salmon adds a smoky char that perfectly complements the citrusy profile. Serve this dish with a side of quinoa or a fresh green salad for a wholesome and refreshing meal that captures the essence of summer.

TOTAL TIME COOKING: 30 minutes

Ingredients:

*   4 salmon fillets

*   1/4 cup olive oil

*   2 cloves garlic, minced

*   1 teaspoon lemon zest

*   1 teaspoon orange zest

*   2 tablespoons fresh lemon juice

*   2 tablespoons fresh orange juice

*   1 tablespoon Dijon mustard

*   Salt and pepper to taste

*   Fresh parsley for garnish

Directions:

1.   Preheat the grill to medium-high heat.

2.   whisk together olive oil, minced garlic, lemon zest, orange zest, lemon juice, orange juice, Dijon mustard, salt, and pepper in a small bowl.

3.   Place the salmon fillets on a plate and brush both sides with the citrus marinade.

4.   Place the salmon fillets on the preheated grill and cook for about 4-5 minutes per side until the salmon is cooked through and easily flakes with a fork.

5.   Remove the salmon from the grill and garnish with fresh parsley.

6.   Enjoy the grilled citrus salmon with your favorite side dishes!

Creamy Salmon Chowder

Transitioning from salads to soul-warming soups, our Creamy Salmon Chowder takes center stage. Velvety and rich, this chowder features chunks of succulent salmon swimming in a creamy broth with potatoes, vegetables, and aromatic herbs. It's a comforting bowl that brings warmth and satisfaction, perfect for chilly evenings.

TOTAL TIME COOKING: 40 minutes

Ingredients:

- 1 pound salmon fillets, skinless and boneless, cut into chunks
- 2 tablespoons butter
- 1 onion, diced
- 2 carrots, diced
- 2 celery stalks, diced
- 3 potatoes, peeled and diced
- 3 cups fish or vegetable broth
- 1 cup corn kernels
- 1 cup milk
- 1/2 cup heavy cream
- 2 tablespoons all-purpose flour
- Salt and black pepper to taste
- Fresh dill, chopped, for garnish

Directions:

1. In a large pot, melt butter over medium heat. Add diced onion, carrots, and celery. Sauté until vegetables are softened.
2. Sprinkle flour over the vegetables and stir to coat.
3. Gradually add fish or vegetable broth, stirring constantly to avoid lumps.
4. Add diced potatoes, corn, milk, and heavy cream to the pot. Bring to a simmer.
5. Gently add salmon chunks to the soup until the salmon is cooked for about 5-7 minutes.

6. Season with salt and black pepper to taste.
7. Serve hot, garnished with chopped fresh dill.

Thai Coconut Salmon Soup

Embark on a culinary journey to Thailand with our Thai Coconut Salmon Soup. The richness of coconut milk, combined with Thai herbs and spices, creates a fragrant and flavorful soup. The tender chunks of salmon add a luxurious touch, making this soup a Thai-inspired delight.

TOTAL TIME COOKING: 30 minutes

Ingredients:

- 1 pound salmon fillets, skinless and boneless, cut into chunks
- 1 tablespoon vegetable oil
- 2 tablespoons red curry paste
- 1 can (14 oz) coconut milk
- 3 cups chicken or fish broth
- 1 red bell pepper, sliced
- 1 zucchini, sliced
- 1 tablespoon fish sauce
- 1 tablespoon soy sauce
- 1 tablespoon brown sugar
- Juice of 1 lime
- Fresh cilantro, chopped, for garnish

Directions:

1. In a large pot, heat vegetable oil over medium heat. Add red curry paste and sauté for 1-2 minutes.
2. Pour in coconut milk and broth, stirring to combine.
3. Add sliced red bell pepper and zucchini to the pot. Simmer until vegetables are tender.
4. Add salmon chunks, fish sauce, soy sauce, brown sugar, and lime juice. Cook until the salmon is cooked through, about 5 minutes.
5. Adjust seasoning if needed.
6. Serve hot, garnished with chopped fresh cilantro.

Lemon Dill Salmon Soup

Refresh your palate with the Lemon Dill Salmon Soup. The bright and citrusy notes of lemon and aromatic dill complement the tender salmon in a light and comforting broth. This soup is perfect for those seeking a soothing and rejuvenating dining experience.

TOTAL TIME COOKING: 25 minutes

Ingredients:

- 1 pound salmon fillets, skinless and boneless, cut into chunks
- 2 tablespoons olive oil
- 1 onion, diced
- 2 carrots, sliced
- 2 celery stalks, sliced
- 4 cups chicken or vegetable broth
- 1 cup orzo pasta
- Zest and juice of 1 lemon
- 1/4 cup fresh dill, chopped
- Salt and black pepper to taste

Directions:

1. In a large pot, heat olive oil over medium heat. Add diced onion, sliced carrots, and celery. Sauté until vegetables are softened.
2. Pour in chicken or vegetable broth and bring to a simmer.
3. Add orzo pasta to the pot and cook until al dente.
4. Gently add salmon chunks, lemon zest, and lemon juice. Cook until the salmon is cooked through, about 5 minutes.
5. Season with salt and black pepper to taste.
6. Stir in chopped fresh dill before serving.

Smoked Salmon and Potato Soup

Experience the smoky richness of smoked salmon in our Smoked Salmon and Potato Soup. The hearty combination of potatoes, vegetables, and smoked salmon creates a robust and satisfying soup. It's a comforting bowl that pays homage to the classic flavors of smoked salmon.

TOTAL TIME COOKING: 35 minutes

Ingredients:

- 1/2 pound smoked salmon, flaked
- 2 tablespoons butter
- 1 onion, diced
- 2 leeks, sliced
- 3 potatoes, peeled and diced
- 4 cups chicken or vegetable broth
- 1 cup milk
- 1/2 cup heavy cream
- Salt and black pepper to taste
- Chives, chopped, for garnish

Directions:

1. In a large pot, melt butter over medium heat. Add diced onion and sliced leeks. Sauté until vegetables are softened.
2. Add diced potatoes and pour in chicken or vegetable broth. Bring to a simmer.
3. Cook until the potatoes are tender.
4. Add flaked smoked salmon, milk, and heavy cream to the pot. Heat through without boiling.
5. Season with salt and black pepper to taste.
6. Serve hot, garnished with chopped chives.

Tuscan White Bean and Salmon Soup

Experience the rustic charm of Italy with our Tuscan White Bean and Salmon Soup. This hearty soup combines the richness of salmon with the earthiness of white beans, creating a wholesome and satisfying dish. Infused with Italian herbs and spices, this soup is a comforting bowl that captures the essence of Tuscan cuisine.

TOTAL TIME COOKING: 40 minutes

Ingredients:

- 1 pound salmon fillets, skinless and boneless, cut into chunks
- 2 tablespoons olive oil
- 1 onion, diced
- 3 cloves garlic, minced
- 2 carrots, diced
- 2 celery stalks, diced
- 2 cans (15 oz each) white beans, drained and rinsed
- 4 cups chicken or vegetable broth
- 1 can (14 oz) diced tomatoes
- 1 teaspoon dried oregano
- 1 teaspoon dried thyme
- Salt and black pepper to taste
- Fresh parsley, chopped, for garnish

Directions:

1. In a large pot, heat olive oil over medium heat. Add diced onion, minced garlic, diced carrots, and diced celery. Sauté until vegetables are softened.
2. Pour in chicken or vegetable broth and bring to a simmer.
3. Add white beans, diced tomatoes, dried oregano, and thyme to the pot. Simmer for 15-20 minutes.
4. Gently add salmon chunks until the salmon is cooked through, about 5 minutes.

5. Season with salt and black pepper to taste. Serve with garnished with chopped fresh parsley.

Coconut Lime Salmon Soup

Our Coconut Lime Salmon Soup takes your taste buds on a tropical escape. The luxurious combination of coconut milk, zesty lime, and tender salmon creates a fragrant and flavorful soup. This exotic blend transports you to a beachside paradise, offering a refreshing twist on traditional salmon soups.

TOTAL TIME COOKING: 30 minutes

Ingredients:

- 1 pound salmon fillets, skinless and boneless, cut into chunks
- 1 tablespoon vegetable oil
- 1 onion, diced
- 3 cloves garlic, minced
- 1 red bell pepper, sliced
- 1 can (14 oz) coconut milk
- 4 cups chicken or fish broth
- Juice of 2 limes
- 1 tablespoon fish sauce
- 1 tablespoon soy sauce
- 1 tablespoon brown sugar
- 1 tablespoon red curry paste
- Fresh cilantro, chopped, for garnish

Directions:

1. In a large pot, heat vegetable oil over medium heat. Add diced onion, minced garlic, and sliced red bell pepper. Sauté until vegetables are softened.
2. Stir in red curry paste and cook for 1-2 minutes.
3. Pour coconut milk, chicken or fish broth, lime juice, fish sauce, soy sauce, and brown sugar. Bring to a simmer.
4. Gently add salmon chunks until the salmon is cooked through, about 5 minutes.

5. Adjust seasoning if needed. Serve hot, garnished with chopped fresh cilantro.

Salmon and Corn Chowder

Indulge in the comforting goodness of our Salmon and Corn Chowder. Creamy and rich, this chowder features succulent salmon, sweet corn, and a medley of vegetables, creating a harmonious blend of flavors. Perfectly seasoned, this chowder is a cozy and satisfying bowl for any occasion.

TOTAL TIME COOKING: 35 minutes

Ingredients:

- 1 pound salmon fillets, skinless and boneless, cut into chunks
- 2 tablespoons butter
- 1 onion, diced
- 2 potatoes, peeled and diced
- 3 cups chicken or vegetable broth
- 1 can (14 oz) creamed corn
- 1 cup frozen corn kernels
- 1 cup milk
- 1/2 cup heavy cream
- Salt and black pepper to taste
- Chives, chopped, for garnish

Directions:

1. In a large pot, melt butter over medium heat. Add diced onion and sauté until softened.
2. Add diced potatoes, chicken or vegetable broth, creamed corn, and frozen kernels. Bring to a simmer.
3. Cook until the potatoes are tender.
4. Gently add salmon chunks, milk, and heavy cream. Cook until the salmon is cooked through, about 5 minutes.
5. Season with salt and black pepper to taste.
6. Serve hot, garnished with chopped chives.

Salmon and Vegetable Miso Soup

Experience the umami goodness of our Salmon and Vegetable Miso Soup. This Japanese-inspired creation combines the delicate flavors of salmon with the depth of miso broth and an array of fresh vegetables. The result is a nourishing and flavorful soup that pays homage to the art of Japanese cuisine.

TOTAL TIME COOKING: 25 minutes

Ingredients:

- 1 pound salmon fillets, skinless and boneless, cut into chunks
- 4 cups dashi (Japanese soup stock)
- 2 tablespoons miso paste
- 1 carrot, julienned
- 1 daikon radish, julienned
- 1 cup snow peas, trimmed
- 2 green onions, sliced
- 1 tablespoon soy sauce
- 1 tablespoon mirin
- 1 tablespoon sake

Directions:

1. In a pot, bring dashi to a simmer.
2. Dissolve miso paste in a ladleful of dashi, then add it to the pot.
3. Add julienned carrot and daikon radish to the pot. Simmer until vegetables are tender.
4. Gently add salmon chunks, snow peas, sliced green onions, soy sauce, mirin, and sake. Cook until the salmon is cooked through, about 5 minutes.
5. Serve hot.

Smoky Salmon and Lentil Soup

Savor the smoky notes in our Smoky Salmon and Lentil Soup. The hearty combination of lentils, vegetables, and smoked salmon creates a robust, comforting, nutritious soup. This soup celebrates wholesome ingredients and bold flavors that will warm your soul.

TOTAL TIME COOKING: 40 minutes

Ingredients:

- 1/2 pound smoked salmon, flaked
- 1 cup dried green or brown lentils, rinsed
- 1 onion, diced
- 2 carrots, diced
- 2 celery stalks, diced
- 3 cloves garlic, minced
- 6 cups chicken or vegetable broth
- 1 teaspoon smoked paprika
- 1 teaspoon cumin
- Salt and black pepper to taste
- Fresh parsley, chopped, for garnish

Directions:

1. In a large pot, combine lentils, diced onion, carrots, celery, minced garlic, chicken or vegetable broth, smoked paprika, and cumin.
2. Bring to a simmer and cook until lentils are tender.
3. Stir in flaked smoked salmon and cook until heated through.
4. Season with salt and black pepper to taste.
5. Serve hot, garnished with chopped fresh parsley.

Salmon and Wild Rice Soup

Elevate your soup experience with our Salmon and Wild Rice Soup. The nutty flavor of wild rice complements the tender chunks of salmon in a broth enriched with vegetables and herbs. This soup is a delicious and wholesome option that showcases the natural goodness of wild rice and salmon.

TOTAL TIME COOKING: 45 minutes

Ingredients:

- 1 pound salmon fillets, skinless and boneless, cut into chunks
- 1 cup wild rice, cooked
- 2 tablespoons olive oil
- 1 onion, diced
- 2 carrots, diced
- 2 celery stalks, diced
- 3 cloves garlic, minced
- 6 cups chicken or vegetable broth
- 1 cup mushrooms, sliced
- 1 cup spinach leaves
- 1 cup half-and-half
- Salt and black pepper to taste
- Fresh dill, chopped, for garnish

Directions:

1. In a large pot, heat olive oil over medium heat. Add diced onion, diced carrots, diced celery, and minced garlic. Sauté until vegetables are softened.
2. Pour in chicken or vegetable broth and bring to a simmer.
3. Add sliced mushrooms, cooked wild rice, and salmon chunks to the pot. Cook until the salmon is cooked through, about 5 minutes.
4. Stir in spinach leaves and half-and-half. Cook until spinach is wilted.
5. Season with salt and black pepper to taste.

6. Serve hot, garnished with chopped fresh dill.

Baked Honey Mustard Glazed Salmon

The Baked Honey Mustard Glazed Salmon is a must-try for a sweet and savory sensation. This menu combines honey's richness and mustard's tanginess to create a luscious glaze that perfectly coats the salmon fillets. The baking process allows the glaze to caramelize, creating a mouthwatering crust that enhances the natural flavors of the salmon. Serve this dish with roasted vegetables or a bed of wild rice to complete the experience. The result is a sophisticated, comforting dish that impresses your guests.

TOTAL TIME COOKING: 25 minutes

Ingredients:

- 4 salmon fillets
- 1/4 cup Dijon mustard
- 2 tablespoons honey
- 2 tablespoons soy sauce
- 1 tablespoon olive oil
- 2 cloves garlic, minced
- 1 teaspoon dried thyme
- Salt and pepper to taste
- Lemon wedges for serving

Directions:

1.   Preheat the oven to 400°F (200°C) and line a baking sheet with parchment paper.

2.   whisk together Dijon mustard, honey, soy sauce, olive oil, minced garlic, dried thyme, salt, and pepper in a small bowl.

3.   Place the salmon fillets on the prepared baking sheet and brush the honey mustard glaze over each fillet.

4.   Bake in the oven for 15-18 minutes or until the salmon is cooked and easily flakes with a fork.

5.   Optional: Broil for 2-3 minutes to achieve a caramelized glaze on top.

6.   Remove the salmon from the oven and squeeze fresh lemon juice over it before serving.

7.   Serve the baked honey mustard glazed salmon with your favorite side dishes for a delightful meal!

Lemon Herb Grilled Salmon

Elevate your grilling game with the Lemon Herb Grilled Salmon, a classic combination that never fails to impress. The marinade, featuring fresh lemon juice, garlic, and a medley of rosemary and thyme, infuses the salmon with aromatic and savory goodness. The grilling process imparts a smoky flavor while maintaining the salmon's natural tenderness. Pair this dish with a light couscous salad or steamed asparagus for a well-rounded meal that showcases the timeless appeal of lemon and herbs.

TOTAL TIME COOKING: 20 minutes

Ingredients:

- 4 salmon fillets
- 1/4 cup olive oil
- 2 tablespoons fresh lemon juice
- 2 cloves garlic, minced
- 1 teaspoon dried oregano
- 1 teaspoon dried thyme
- Salt and pepper to taste
- Lemon wedges for serving
- Fresh parsley for garnish

Directions:

1. Preheat the grill to medium-high heat.

2. whisk together olive oil, fresh lemon juice, minced garlic, dried oregano, dried thyme, salt, and pepper in a small bowl.

3. Place the salmon fillets on a plate and brush both sides with the lemon herb marinade.

4.   Grill the salmon for about 3-4 minutes per side or until it is cooked to your desired doneness.

5.   Remove from the grill, garnish with fresh parsley, and serve with lemon wedges.

Teriyaki Glazed Grilled Salmon

Transport yourself to the streets of Tokyo with our Teriyaki Glazed Grilled Salmon. The sweet and savory teriyaki glaze caramelizes on the grill, creating a perfect balance of flavors. The result is a succulent salmon dish that effortlessly blends the richness of teriyaki with the smoky essence of grilling. Serve with steamed rice or stir-fried vegetables for an authentic Asian-inspired feast.

TOTAL TIME COOKING: 25 minutes

Ingredients:

- 4 salmon fillets
- 1/2 cup teriyaki sauce
- 2 tablespoons honey
- 1 tablespoon sesame oil
- 2 cloves garlic, minced
- 1 teaspoon grated ginger
- Sesame seeds for garnish
- Green onions, chopped, for garnish

Directions:

1. Preheat the grill to medium heat.

2. Mix teriyaki sauce, honey, sesame oil, minced garlic, and grated ginger in a bowl to make the teriyaki glaze.

3. Place salmon fillets on the grill and brush with the teriyaki glaze.

4. Grill for 4-5 minutes per side, basting with additional glaze as needed.

5. Remove from the grill, sprinkle with sesame seeds and chopped green onions, and serve.

Maple Dijon Grilled Salmon

Indulge in the sweet and tangy symphony of flavors with our Maple Dijon Grilled Salmon. The combination of maple syrup and Dijon mustard creates a delectable glaze that enhances the natural richness of the salmon. The grilling process adds a smoky touch, making it a sophisticated and irresistible dish. Pair with roasted sweet potatoes or a fresh arugula salad for a delightful culinary experience.

TOTAL TIME COOKING: 22 minutes

Ingredients:

- 4 salmon fillets
- 1/4 cup maple syrup
- 2 tablespoons Dijon mustard
- 1 tablespoon soy sauce
- 1 tablespoon olive oil
- 2 cloves garlic, minced
- Salt and pepper to taste

Directions:

1. Preheat the grill to medium-high heat.

2. whisk together maple syrup, Dijon mustard, soy sauce, olive oil, minced garlic, salt, and pepper in a small bowl.

3. Brush the salmon fillets with the maple Dijon mixture.

4. Grill the salmon for approximately 4-5 minutes per side or until it flakes easily with a fork.

5. Serve immediately and enjoy the sweet and savory flavors.

Cajun Spiced Grilled Salmon

Add a kick to your palate with our Cajun Spiced Grilled Salmon. The bold Cajun seasoning infuses the salmon with a smoky, spicy flavor that takes your taste buds to the heart of Louisiana. Grilling enhances the smokiness and adds a satisfying char to the salmon. Serve with a side of dirty rice or cornbread for a Southern-inspired feast.

TOTAL TIME COOKING: 18 minutes

Ingredients:

- 4 salmon fillets
- 2 tablespoons Cajun seasoning
- 2 tablespoons olive oil
- 1 teaspoon paprika
- 1 teaspoon garlic powder
- 1 teaspoon onion powder
- Salt and pepper to taste
- Lemon wedges for serving

Directions:

1. Preheat the grill to medium-high heat.

2. mix Cajun seasoning, olive oil, paprika, garlic powder, onion powder, salt, and pepper to create a spice rub.

3. Rub the spice mixture evenly over both sides of the salmon fillets.

4. Grill the salmon for about 3-4 minutes per side or until it reaches your desired level of doneness.

5. Serve with lemon wedges for an extra burst of flavor.

Mediterranean Grilled Salmon

Savor the flavors of the Mediterranean with our Grilled Salmon infused with olive oil, lemon, garlic, and a medley of herbs. This menu combines the freshness of Mediterranean ingredients with the smokiness of grilling, creating a light and satisfying dish. Serve over couscous or with a Greek salad for a taste of the sunny Mediterranean coast.

TOTAL TIME COOKING: 30 minutes

Ingredients:

*   4 salmon fillets

*   1/4 cup olive oil

*   2 tablespoons lemon juice

*   2 teaspoons dried oregano

*   1 teaspoon dried basil

*   1 teaspoon minced garlic

*   1/2 teaspoon smoked paprika

*   Salt and pepper to taste

*   Kalamata olives and cherry tomatoes for garnish

Directions:

1.   Preheat the grill to medium heat.

2.   whisk olive oil, lemon juice, dried oregano, dried basil, minced garlic, smoked paprika, salt, and pepper in a small bowl.

3.   Brush the salmon fillets with the Mediterranean marinade.

4.   Grill the salmon for 4-5 minutes per side or until it flakes easily with a fork.

5.   Garnish with Kalamata olives and cherry tomatoes before serving for a taste of the Mediterranean.

Grilled Salmon Tacos with Avocado Crema

Try our Grilled Salmon Tacos with Avocado Crema for a fusion of flavors. The grilled salmon, combined with the creaminess of avocado crema, creates a satisfying and refreshing taco. Top with shredded cabbage, pico de gallo, and a squeeze of lime for an extra burst of flavor. It's the perfect choice for a casual and delightful meal.

TOTAL TIME COOKING: 25 minutes

Ingredients:

- 1 pound salmon fillets
- 1 tablespoon olive oil
- 1 teaspoon chili powder
- 1 teaspoon cumin
- Salt and pepper to taste
- 8 small flour or corn tortillas
- Shredded cabbage or lettuce
- Diced tomatoes
- Fresh cilantro, chopped
- Lime wedges

Directions:

1. Preheat the grill to medium-high heat.

2. Rub salmon fillets with olive oil, chili powder, cumin, salt, and pepper.

3. Grill salmon for 4-5 minutes per side or until cooked through.

4. Flake the salmon into chunks.

5. Warm tortillas on the grill.

6.   Assemble tacos with shredded cabbage or lettuce, grilled salmon, diced tomatoes, and cilantro.

7.   Drizzle with avocado crema (combine mashed avocado, sour cream, lime juice, salt, and pepper).

8.   Serve with lime wedges on the side.

Teriyaki Salmon Wraps

Experience the perfect balance of sweet and savory with our Teriyaki Salmon Wraps. The teriyaki-glazed grilled salmon is wrapped in a tortilla with fresh vegetables and a drizzle of teriyaki sauce, creating a handheld delight. This menu is ideal for those on the go who still crave a gourmet experience.

TOTAL TIME COOKING: 20 minutes

Ingredients:

- 1 pound salmon fillets

- 1/4 cup teriyaki sauce

- 4 large whole wheat or spinach tortillas

- 1 cup shredded carrots

- 1 cucumber, julienned

- 1 avocado, sliced

- Sesame seeds for garnish

- Green onions, chopped, for garnish

Directions:

1.   Preheat the oven to 400°F (200°C).

2.   Brush salmon fillets with teriyaki sauce and bake for 15-18 minutes or until cooked.

3.   Flake the salmon into bite-sized pieces.

4.   Warm the tortillas.

5.   Assemble wraps with salmon, shredded carrots, julienned cucumber, and avocado slices.

6.   Sprinkle with sesame seeds and chopped green onions.

7.   Fold and secure with toothpicks if necessary.

8.   Serve immediately.

Smoked Salmon and Cream Cheese Tacos

Elevate your taco game with our Smoked Salmon and Cream Cheese Tacos. The smoky richness of the salmon pairs beautifully with the creamy texture of the cream cheese, creating a luxurious taco experience. Top with capers, red onion, and fresh dill for elegance.

TOTAL TIME COOKING: 15 minutes

Ingredients:

- 8 small flour or corn tortillas
- 8 ounces smoked salmon
- 4 ounces cream cheese, softened
- Red onion, thinly sliced
- Capers
- Fresh dill, chopped
- Lemon wedges

Directions:

1. Warm the tortillas.
2. Spread a layer of cream cheese onto each tortilla.
3. Top with smoked salmon, red onion slices, capers, and fresh dill.
4. Squeeze lemon juice over the top.
5. Fold the tacos and serve immediately.

Cajun Salmon Tacos with Mango Salsa

For a tropical twist, try our Cajun Salmon Tacos with Mango Salsa. The sweet and tangy mango salsa perfectly complements the spicy Cajun-seasoned salmon. These tacos are a burst of flavors that transport you to a Caribbean paradise. Top with cilantro and a squeeze of lime for a finishing touch.

TOTAL TIME COOKING: 30 minutes

Ingredients:

- 1 pound salmon fillets

- 1 tablespoon Cajun seasoning

- 8 small flour or corn tortillas

- Shredded lettuce

- Mango salsa (diced mango, red onion, cilantro, lime juice)

- Greek yogurt or sour cream for topping

Directions:

1. Preheat the oven to 400°F (200°C).

2. Rub salmon fillets with Cajun seasoning and bake for 15-18 minutes or until cooked.

3. Flake the salmon into chunks.

4. Warm the tortillas.

5. Assemble tacos with shredded lettuce, Cajun salmon, and mango salsa.

6. Top with a dollop of Greek yogurt or sour cream.

7. Serve immediately.

Greek Salmon Pita Wraps

Experience the flavors of Greece with our Greek Salmon Pita Wraps. The grilled salmon, marinated in olive oil, lemon, and Mediterranean herbs, is wrapped in warm pita bread with tzatziki sauce, cucumber, and feta cheese. It's a light and refreshing option that brings the taste of the Aegean to your table.

TOTAL TIME COOKING: 25 minutes

Ingredients:

- 1 pound salmon fillets
- 4 whole wheat pita bread
- Tzatziki sauce
- Cherry tomatoes, halved
- Cucumber, sliced
- Red onion, thinly sliced
- Kalamata olives, sliced
- Feta cheese, crumbled
- Fresh parsley, chopped

Directions:

1. Preheat the grill to medium-high heat.

2. Grill salmon for 4-5 minutes per side or until cooked through.

3. Flake the salmon into bite-sized pieces.

4. Warm the pita bread.

5. Spread a layer of tzatziki sauce on each pita.

6. Assemble wraps with grilled salmon, cherry tomatoes, cucumber slices, red onion slices, Kalamata olives, feta cheese, and fresh parsley.

Southwest Salmon Tacos with Chipotle Lime Crema

Spice up your taco night with our Southwest Salmon Tacos featuring Chipotle Lime Crema. The salmon is seasoned with Southwest spices, perfectly grilled, and topped with a zesty chipotle lime crema. Pair with black bean salsa and avocado for a fiesta of flavors that will leave your taste buds dancing.

TOTAL TIME COOKING: 25 minutes

Ingredients:

- 1 pound salmon fillets
- 1 tablespoon olive oil
- 1 tablespoon taco seasoning
- 8 small corn or flour tortillas
- Shredded lettuce
- Black beans, drained and rinsed
- Corn kernels (fresh or frozen)
- Avocado, sliced
- Chipotle Lime Crema (mix sour cream, chipotle in adobo sauce, lime juice, salt)

Directions:

1. Preheat the oven to 400°F (200°C).

2. Rub salmon fillets with olive oil and taco seasoning. Bake for 15-18 minutes or until cooked through.

3. Flake the salmon into chunks.

4. Warm the tortillas.

5.   Assemble tacos with shredded lettuce, black beans, corn, sliced avocado, and flaked salmon.

6.   Drizzle with chipotle lime crema.

7.   Serve immediately.

Asian-Inspired Salmon Spring Rolls

Embark on a journey to the Far East with our Asian-Inspired Salmon Spring Rolls. The delicate balance of fresh salmon, crisp vegetables, and aromatic herbs wrapped in rice paper creates a light and flavorful appetizer. Pair with a savory dipping sauce for an authentic and refreshing start to your culinary adventure.

TOTAL TIME COOKING: 20 minutes

Ingredients:

- 1 pound salmon fillets, poached and flaked
- Rice paper wrappers
- Rice noodles, cooked
- Carrots, julienned
- Cucumber, julienned
- Fresh mint leaves
- Sesame seeds for garnish
- Hoisin-peanut dipping sauce

Directions:

1. Prepare all the ingredients.

2. Soften rice paper wrappers in warm water.

3. Lay a wrapper flat and add some salmon, rice noodles, carrots, cucumber, and mint leaves.

4. Roll tightly, folding in the sides.

5. Repeat for remaining ingredients.

6. Sprinkle with sesame seeds.

7. Serve with hoisin-peanut dipping sauce.

Grilled Pineapple and Salmon Tacos

Experience a tropical fiesta with our Grilled Pineapple and Salmon Tacos. The smoky grilled salmon and sweet, caramelized pineapple create a symphony of flavors in each bite. Top with cilantro, red onion, and a drizzle of lime for a taco that transports your taste buds to a sun-soaked paradise.

TOTAL TIME COOKING: 30 minutes

Ingredients:

- 1 pound salmon fillets
- 8 small corn or flour tortillas
- 1 cup diced pineapple, grilled
- Red cabbage, thinly sliced
- Jalapeño, thinly sliced
- Cilantro, chopped
- Lime wedges
- Creamy avocado dressing

Directions:

1. Preheat the grill to medium-high heat.

2. Grill salmon for 4-5 minutes per side or until cooked through.

3. Warm the tortillas.

4. Assemble tacos with grilled salmon, pineapple, sliced red cabbage, jalapeño, and cilantro.

5. Squeeze lime juice over the top.

6. Drizzle with creamy avocado dressing.

7. Serve immediately.

Mediterranean Salmon Gyro Wrap

Indulge in the rich flavors of the Mediterranean with our Salmon Gyro Wrap. Grilled salmon, marinated in Mediterranean herbs and spices, is wrapped in warm pita bread with tzatziki sauce, tomatoes, and cucumber. It's a taste of the Aegean that brings freshness and savory satisfaction together.

TOTAL TIME COOKING: 25 minutes

Ingredients:

- 1 pound salmon fillets

- 4 whole wheat flatbreads or pitas

- Tzatziki sauce

- Red onion, thinly sliced

- Tomato, diced

- Cucumber, sliced

- Kalamata olives, sliced

- Feta cheese, crumbled

- Fresh dill, chopped

Directions:

1. Preheat the grill to medium-high heat.

2. Grill salmon for 4-5 minutes per side or until cooked through.

3. Flake the salmon into chunks.

4. Warm the flatbreads or pitas.

5. Spread a layer of tzatziki sauce on each.

6. Assemble wraps with grilled salmon, red onion slices, diced tomato, cucumber slices, Kalamata olives, feta cheese, and fresh dill.

7.   Roll and serve immediately.

Coconut Lime Salmon Tacos

Transport yourself to a beachside paradise with our Coconut Lime Salmon Tacos. The tropical fusion of coconut and lime enhances the natural sweetness of salmon, creating a delightful taco experience. Top with shredded cabbage and a drizzle of coconut-lime crema to taste the tropics.

TOTAL TIME COOKING: 20 minutes

Ingredients:

- 1 pound salmon fillets
- 1/2 cup coconut milk
- Zest and juice of 1 lime
- 2 tablespoons coconut flakes, toasted
- 8 small corn or flour tortillas
- Shredded lettuce
- Pineapple salsa (diced pineapple, red onion, cilantro, lime juice)
- Avocado slices

Directions:

1. Preheat the oven to 400°F (200°C).

2. Combine coconut milk, lime zest, and lime juice.

3. Place salmon fillets in a baking dish, pour coconut-lime mixture over them and bake for 15-18 minutes.

4. Flake the salmon into chunks.

5. Warm the tortillas.

6. Assemble tacos with shredded lettuce, coconut-lime salmon, pineapple salsa, toasted coconut flakes, and avocado slices.

7. Serve immediately.

Creamy Lemon Garlic Salmon Pasta

Indulge in a velvety pasta dish with our Creamy Lemon Garlic Salmon Pasta. The richness of the creamy sauce, infused with lemon and garlic, complements the succulent salmon. Tossed with al dente pasta, this dish is a harmonious blend of comfort and sophistication.

TOTAL TIME COOKING: 25 minutes

Ingredients:

- 8 oz (225g) pasta of your choice
- 1 pound salmon fillets, skinless and boneless
- Salt and black pepper to taste
- 2 tablespoons olive oil
- 4 cloves garlic, minced
- 1 cup cherry tomatoes, halved
- 1/2 cup chicken or vegetable broth
- 1 cup heavy cream
- Zest and juice of 1 lemon
- 1/4 cup fresh parsley, chopped
- Grated Parmesan cheese for garnish

Directions:

1.   Cook the pasta according to package instructions. Drain and set aside.

2.   Season the salmon fillets with salt and black pepper.

3.   In a large skillet, heat olive oil over medium-high heat. Add salmon and sear for 3-4 minutes per side until cooked. Remove and set aside.

4.   In the same skillet, add minced garlic and cherry tomatoes. Sauté until tomatoes are softened.

5.   Pour the broth and heavy cream, then add lemon zest and juice. Stir to combine.

6.   Slice the seared salmon into bite-sized pieces and add them to the skillet.

7.   Add the cooked pasta and toss everything together until well-coated.

8.   Sprinkle with chopped parsley and Parmesan cheese before serving.

Spicy Tomato Basil Salmon Pasta

Ignite your taste buds with our Spicy Tomato Basil Salmon Pasta. The bold combination of spicy tomatoes, aromatic basil, and perfectly grilled salmon creates a pasta dish that is both vibrant and satisfying. A touch of red pepper flakes adds a kick to this flavorful ensemble.

TOTAL TIME COOKING: 30 minutes

Ingredients:

- 8 oz (225g) pasta of your choice
- 1 pound salmon fillets, skinless and boneless
- Salt and black pepper to taste
- 2 tablespoons olive oil
- 1 onion, finely chopped
- 3 cloves garlic, minced
- 1 can (14 oz) diced tomatoes
- 1 teaspoon red pepper flakes (adjust to taste)
- 1 teaspoon dried basil
- 1/2 cup heavy cream
- Grated Parmesan cheese for serving

Directions:

1. Cook the pasta according to package instructions. Drain and set aside.

2. Season the salmon fillets with salt and black pepper.

3. In a large skillet, heat olive oil over medium heat. Add chopped onion and sauté until softened.

4. Add minced garlic and sauté for 1-2 minutes.

5.   Place the salmon fillets in the skillet and cook for 3-4 minutes per side until done. Remove and flake into bite-sized pieces.

6.   Add diced tomatoes, red pepper flakes, and dried basil to the skillet. Stir and cook for 5 minutes.

7.   Pour in the heavy cream and stir until well combined.

8.   Add the cooked pasta and flaked salmon, tossing to coat in the sauce.

9.   Serve with grated Parmesan cheese on top.

Pesto Cream Salmon Pasta

Delight in the classic flavors of pesto with our Pesto Cream Salmon Pasta. The aromatic blend of fresh basil, pine nuts, and Parmesan, combined with the creamy richness of the sauce, enhances the grilled salmon. This pasta dish is a celebration of simplicity and taste.

TOTAL TIME COOKING: 20 minutes

Ingredients:

- 8 oz (225g) fettuccine pasta
- 1 pound salmon fillets, skinless and boneless
- Salt and black pepper to taste
- 2 tablespoons olive oil
- 1/2 cup pesto sauce
- 1 cup cherry tomatoes, halved
- 1/2 cup heavy cream
- Grated Parmesan cheese for serving

Directions:

1.   Cook the fettuccine pasta according to package instructions. Drain and set aside.

2.   Season the salmon fillets with salt and black pepper.

3.   In a large skillet, heat olive oil over medium-high heat. Add salmon and sear for 3-4 minutes per side until cooked. Remove and set aside.

4.   In the same skillet, add pesto sauce and cherry tomatoes. Sauté for 2-3 minutes.

5.   Pour in the heavy cream and stir until well combined.

6.   Slice the seared salmon into bite-sized pieces and add them to the skillet.

7.   Add the cooked fettuccine pasta and toss everything together until well-coated.

8.   Serve with grated Parmesan cheese on top.

Garlic Butter Salmon and Asparagus Pasta

Savor the luxurious combination of garlic butter, tender asparagus, and grilled salmon with our Garlic Butter Salmon and Asparagus Pasta. This dish showcases the delicate balance of flavors, creating a comforting and elegant pasta experience.

TOTAL TIME COOKING: 30 minutes

Ingredients:

- 8 oz (225g) linguine or spaghetti
- 1 pound salmon fillets, skinless and boneless
- Salt and black pepper to taste
- 3 tablespoons unsalted butter
- 4 cloves garlic, minced
- 1 bunch of asparagus, trimmed and cut into bite-sized pieces
- Zest and juice of 1 lemon
- 1/2 cup chicken or vegetable broth
- Grated Parmesan cheese for serving

Directions:

1. Cook the pasta according to package instructions. Drain and set aside.

2. Season the salmon fillets with salt and black pepper.

3. In a large skillet, melt butter over medium heat. Add minced garlic and sauté until fragrant.

4. Add salmon fillets to the skillet and cook for 3-4 minutes per side until done. Remove and set aside.

5. In the same skillet, add asparagus and sauté until tender-crisp.

6. Pour in the chicken or vegetable broth and simmer.

7. Slice the seared salmon into bite-sized pieces and add them back to the skillet.

8. Add the cooked pasta, lemon zest, and lemon juice. Toss everything together until well coated.

9. Serve with grated Parmesan cheese on top.

Creamy Tomato and Spinach Salmon Pasta

Indulge in a wholesome and comforting meal with our Creamy Tomato and Spinach Salmon Pasta. The creamy tomato sauce, paired with nutrient-rich spinach and perfectly cooked salmon, creates a pasta dish that is both hearty and nutritious.

TOTAL TIME COOKING: 25 minutes

Ingredients:

- 8 oz (225g) penne pasta

- 1 pound salmon fillets, skinless and boneless

- Salt and black pepper to taste

- 2 tablespoons olive oil

- 1 onion, finely chopped

- 3 cloves garlic, minced

- 1 can (14 oz) crushed tomatoes

- 1/2 cup heavy cream

- 2 cups fresh spinach

- Grated Parmesan cheese for serving

Directions:

1.   Cook the penne pasta according to package instructions. Drain and set aside.

2.   Season the salmon fillets with salt and black pepper.

3.   In a large skillet, heat olive oil over medium heat. Add chopped onion and sauté until softened.

4.   Add minced garlic and sauté for 1-2 minutes.

5. Place the salmon fillets in the skillet and cook for 3-4 minutes per side until done. Remove and flake into bite-sized pieces.

6. Add crushed tomatoes to the skillet. Stir and cook for 5 minutes.

7. Pour in the heavy cream and stir until well combined.

8. Add fresh spinach and cook until wilted.

9. Add the cooked penne pasta and flaked salmon, tossing to coat in the sauce.

10. Serve with grated Parmesan cheese on top.

Lemon Dill Salmon Alfredo Pasta

Elevate your pasta game with our Lemon Dill Salmon Alfredo Pasta. The zesty freshness of lemon and aromatic dill enhances the creamy Alfredo sauce, creating a pasta dish that is both sophisticated and comforting. The grilled salmon adds a hearty touch to this delectable ensemble.

TOTAL TIME COOKING: 25 minutes

Ingredients:

- 8 oz (225g) fettuccine pasta

- 1 pound salmon fillets, skinless and boneless

- Salt and black pepper to taste

- 2 tablespoons olive oil

- 4 cloves garlic, minced

- 1 cup cherry tomatoes, halved

- 1/2 cup dry white wine (optional)

- 1 cup heavy cream

- Zest and juice of 1 lemon

- 2 tablespoons fresh dill, chopped

- Grated Parmesan cheese for serving

Directions:

1.   Cook the fettuccine pasta according to package instructions. Drain and set aside.

2.   Season the salmon fillets with salt and black pepper.

3.   In a large skillet, heat olive oil over medium-high heat. Add salmon and sear for 3-4 minutes per side until cooked. Remove and set aside.

4. In the same skillet, add minced garlic and cherry tomatoes. Sauté until tomatoes are softened.

5. Pour in the dry white wine (if using) and deglaze the pan, scraping up any browned bits.

6. Add heavy cream, lemon zest, and lemon juice. Stir to combine.

7. Slice the seared salmon into bite-sized pieces and add them to the skillet and fresh dill.

8. Add the cooked fettuccine pasta and toss everything together until well-coated.

9. Serve with grated Parmesan cheese on top.

Sun-dried tomato and Basil Salmon Pasta

Experience the robust flavors of sun-dried tomatoes and basil in our Sun-Dried Tomato and Basil Salmon Pasta. The sweet and tangy notes of sun-dried tomatoes complement the grilled salmon, creating a pasta dish that is both vibrant and satisfying.

TOTAL TIME COOKING: 30 minutes

Ingredients:

- 8 oz (225g) penne pasta

- 1 pound salmon fillets, skinless and boneless

- Salt and black pepper to taste

- 2 tablespoons olive oil

- 1 onion, finely chopped

- 3 cloves garlic, minced

- 1/2 cup sun-dried tomatoes, sliced

- 1 cup cherry tomatoes, halved

- 1 cup chicken or vegetable broth

- 1/2 cup heavy cream

- Fresh basil leaves, chopped

- Grated Parmesan cheese for serving

Directions:

1. Cook the penne pasta according to package instructions. Drain and set aside.

2. Season the salmon fillets with salt and black pepper.

3. In a large skillet, heat olive oil over medium heat. Add chopped onion and sauté until softened.

4.   Add minced garlic and sun-dried tomatoes. Sauté for an additional 2 minutes.

5.   Place the salmon fillets in the skillet and cook for 3-4 minutes per side until done. Remove and set aside.

6.   Add cherry tomatoes to the skillet and cook until softened.

7.   Pour in the chicken or vegetable broth and simmer.

8.   Slice the seared salmon into bite-sized pieces and add them back to the skillet.

9.   Add the cooked penne pasta, heavy cream, and fresh basil. Toss everything together until well coated.

10.   Serve with grated Parmesan cheese on top.

Smoked Salmon and Creamy Pesto Pasta

Indulge in the exquisite combination of smoked salmon and creamy pesto with our Smoked Salmon and Creamy Pesto Pasta. The smoky richness of the salmon pairs perfectly with the basil-infused pesto, creating a pasta dish that is both luxurious and flavorful.

TOTAL TIME COOKING: 20 minutes

Ingredients:

- 8 oz (225g) linguine or spaghetti
- 4 oz smoked salmon, sliced
- 1/2 cup pesto sauce
- 1/2 cup cherry tomatoes, halved
- 1/2 cup heavy cream
- Zest and juice of 1 lemon
- Salt and black pepper to taste
- Fresh parsley, chopped, for garnish
- Grated Parmesan cheese for serving

Directions:

1. Cook the pasta according to package instructions. Drain and set aside.

2. combine smoked salmon, pesto sauce, cherry tomatoes, heavy cream, lemon zest, and lemon juice in a large skillet.

3. Heat over medium heat until the sauce is heated through.

4. Season with salt and black pepper to taste.

5. Add the cooked pasta to the skillet and toss in the creamy pesto sauce until well coated.

6.   Garnish with chopped fresh parsley and serve with grated Parmesan cheese.

Cajun Shrimp and Salmon Pasta

Spice up your pasta night with our Cajun Shrimp and Salmon Pasta. The bold Cajun spices kick the dish, complementing the succulent shrimp and salmon. This pasta celebrates flavors that will leave your taste buds tingling.

TOTAL TIME COOKING: 25 minutes

Ingredients:

- 8 oz (225g) fettuccine pasta
- 1/2 pound shrimp, peeled and deveined
- 1 pound salmon fillets, skinless and boneless
- Cajun seasoning to taste
- 2 tablespoons olive oil
- 4 cloves garlic, minced
- 1 cup cherry tomatoes, halved
- 1/2 cup chicken broth
- 1 cup heavy cream
- Fresh parsley, chopped, for garnish
- Grated Parmesan cheese for serving

Directions:

1. Cook the fettuccine pasta according to package instructions. Drain and set aside.

2. Season shrimp and salmon fillets with Cajun seasoning.

3. In a large skillet, heat olive oil over medium-high heat. Add shrimp and cook for 2-3 minutes per side until opaque. Remove and set aside.

4.   In the same skillet, add minced garlic and cherry tomatoes. Sauté until tomatoes are softened.

5.   Pour in the chicken broth and heavy cream. Stir to combine.

6.   Add the cooked fettuccine pasta, cooked shrimp, and flaked salmon. Toss everything together until well coated.

7.   Garnish with chopped fresh parsley and serve with grated Parmesan cheese.

Mediterranean Salmon and Artichoke Pasta

Embark on a culinary journey to the Mediterranean with our Salmon and Artichoke Pasta. The combination of grilled salmon and marinated artichokes creates a pasta dish that is both hearty and refreshing. The Mediterranean flavors shine through in every bite.

TOTAL TIME COOKING: 30 minutes

Ingredients:

- 8 oz (225g) penne pasta
- 1 pound salmon fillets, skinless and boneless
- Salt and black pepper to taste
- 2 tablespoons olive oil
- 1 onion, finely chopped
- 3 cloves garlic, minced
- 1 can (14 oz) artichoke hearts, drained and quartered
- 1 cup cherry tomatoes, halved
- 1/2 cup Kalamata olives, sliced
- 1/4 cup capers
- 1/2 cup chicken or vegetable broth
- 1/2 cup crumbled feta cheese
- Fresh basil leaves, chopped, for garnish

Directions:

1. Cook the penne pasta according to package instructions. Drain and set aside.

2. Season the salmon fillets with salt and black pepper.

3.   In a large skillet, heat olive oil over medium heat. Add chopped onion and sauté until softened.

4.   Add minced garlic and cook for 1-2 minutes.

5.   Place the salmon fillets in the skillet and cook for 3-4 minutes per side until done. Remove and set aside.

6.   Add artichoke hearts, cherry tomatoes, Kalamata olives, and capers to the skillet. Sauté for 5 minutes.

7.   Pour in the chicken or vegetable broth and simmer.

8.   Slice the seared salmon into bite-sized pieces and add them back to the skillet.

9.   Add the cooked penne pasta and toss everything together until well-coated.

10.   Sprinkle with crumbled feta cheese and chopped fresh basil before serving.

Grilled Salmon Salad with Lemon-Dill Dressing

Refresh your palate with our Grilled Salmon Salad featuring a zesty Lemon-Dill Dressing. The combination of crisp greens, grilled salmon, and a refreshing dressing creates a light and satisfying salad. It's the perfect option for those seeking a healthy and flavorful meal.

TOTAL TIME cooking: 25 minutes

Ingredients:

- 1 pound salmon fillets
- Salt and black pepper to taste
- 8 cups mixed salad greens
- 1 cucumber, sliced
- 1 cup cherry tomatoes, halved
- 1/4 red onion, thinly sliced
- 1/4 cup feta cheese, crumbled
- 1/4 cup fresh dill, chopped

Lemon-Dill Dressing:

- 1/4 cup olive oil
- Zest and juice of 1 lemon
- 1 tablespoon Dijon mustard
- 1 tablespoon honey
- Salt and black pepper to taste

Directions:

1. Season the salmon fillets with salt and black pepper.
2. Grill the salmon for 4-5 minutes per side or until cooked through.
3. In a large bowl, toss salad greens, cucumber, cherry tomatoes, red onion, feta cheese, and chopped dill.
4. Whisk together olive oil, lemon zest, lemon juice, Dijon mustard, honey, salt, and black pepper in a small bowl to make the dressing.

5. Flake the grilled salmon over the salad and drizzle with the lemon-dill dressing.
6. Toss gently to combine and serve immediately.

Citrus Glazed Salmon Salad

Kicking off our culinary adventure is the Citrus Glazed Salmon Salad. The succulent grilled salmon, dressed in a vibrant citrus glaze, takes center stage in this refreshing salad. The crisp greens and a medley of colorful vegetables create a harmonious blend of flavors. The zesty citrus notes add a delightful freshness, making this salad perfect for a light and refreshing meal.

TOTAL TIME cooking: 20 minutes

Ingredients:

- 1 pound salmon fillets
- Salt and black pepper to taste
- 6 cups mixed salad greens
- 1 orange, segmented
- 1 grapefruit, segmented
- 1 avocado, sliced
- 1/4 cup red onion, thinly sliced
- 1/4 cup almonds, toasted and chopped

Citrus Glaze:

- 2 tablespoons honey
- 2 tablespoons orange juice
- 1 tablespoon Dijon mustard
- 1 tablespoon olive oil
- Salt and black pepper to taste

Directions:

1. Season the salmon fillets with salt and black pepper.
2. Whisk together honey, orange juice, Dijon mustard, olive oil, salt, and black pepper in a small bowl to make the citrus glaze.
3. Grill the salmon for 4-5 minutes per side or until cooked through, brushing with the citrus glaze.

4. Arrange salad greens and top with orange and grapefruit segments, sliced avocado, red onion, and toasted almonds in a large bowl.
5. Place the grilled salmon on top and drizzle with the remaining citrus glaze.
6. Serve immediately.

Asian Sesame Salmon Salad

Transport your taste buds to the Far East with the Asian Sesame Salmon Salad. The grilled salmon, marinated in Asian-inspired sesame flavors, harmonizes with crunchy vegetables and crisp greens. Topped with sesame seeds and a drizzle of sesame dressing, this salad is a symphony of textures and tastes that capture the essence of Asian cuisine.

TOTAL TIME cooking: 25 minutes

Ingredients:

- 1 pound salmon fillets
- Salt and black pepper to taste
- 8 cups mixed salad greens
- 1 cup shredded carrots
- 1 cucumber, julienned
- 1/4 cup sliced radishes
- 1/4 cup edamame, steamed
- 2 tablespoons sesame seeds, toasted

Asian Sesame Dressing:

- 3 tablespoons soy sauce
- 2 tablespoons rice vinegar
- 1 tablespoon sesame oil
- 1 tablespoon honey
- 1 teaspoon grated ginger
- 1 clove garlic, minced

Directions:

1. Season the salmon fillets with salt and black pepper.
2. Grill the salmon for 4-5 minutes per side or until cooked through.
3. Combine salad greens, shredded carrots, julienned cucumber, sliced radishes, and edamame in a large bowl.

4. In a small bowl, whisk together soy sauce, rice vinegar, sesame oil, honey, grated ginger, and minced garlic to make the Asian sesame dressing.
5. Flake the grilled salmon over the salad and sprinkle with toasted sesame seeds.
6. Drizzle the salad with the Asian sesame dressing and toss gently to combine.
7. Serve immediately.

Mediterranean Salmon and Quinoa Salad

Indulge in the wholesome goodness of the Mediterranean with our Salmon and Quinoa Salad. Grilled salmon, paired with nutrient-rich quinoa, fresh vegetables, and a lemon-oregano dressing, creates a satisfying and nutritious salad. The Mediterranean flavors shine through, offering a delightful combination of freshness and heartiness.

TOTAL TIME cooking: 30 minutes

Ingredients:

- 1 cup quinoa, cooked
- 1 pound salmon fillets
- Salt and black pepper to taste
- 8 cups mixed salad greens
- 1 cup cherry tomatoes, halved
- 1 cucumber, diced
- 1/4 cup Kalamata olives, sliced
- 1/4 cup feta cheese, crumbled
- Fresh parsley, chopped, for garnish

Mediterranean Dressing:

- 1/4 cup olive oil
- 2 tablespoons red wine vinegar
- 1 teaspoon dried oregano
- Salt and black pepper to taste

Directions:

1. Cook quinoa according to package instructions and let it cool.
2. Season the salmon fillets with salt and black pepper.
3. Grill the salmon for 4-5 minutes per side or until cooked through.
4. Combine salad greens, cooked quinoa, cherry tomatoes, diced cucumber, sliced Kalamata olives, and crumbled feta cheese in a large bowl.

5. In a small bowl, whisk together olive oil, red wine vinegar, dried oregano, salt, and black pepper to make the Mediterranean dressing.
6. Flake the grilled salmon over the salad and drizzle with the Mediterranean dressing.
7. Toss gently to combine and garnish with chopped fresh parsley.
8. Serve immediately.

Avocado and Mango Salmon Salad

Experience a tropical delight with the Avocado and Mango Salmon Salad. The richness of avocado, the sweetness of mango, and the savory grilled salmon create a vibrant and indulgent salad. Tossed with a citrusy vinaigrette, this dish is a perfect blend of flavors that will transport you to a sun-soaked paradise.

TOTAL TIME cooking: 20 minutes

Ingredients:

- 1 pound salmon fillets
- Salt and black pepper to taste
- 6 cups mixed salad greens
- 1 mango, peeled and diced
- 1 avocado, sliced
- 1/4 red onion, thinly sliced
- 1/4 cup chopped cilantro
- 1/4 cup pine nuts, toasted

Citrus Vinaigrette:

- 2 tablespoons orange juice
- 2 tablespoons lime juice
- 2 tablespoons olive oil
- 1 teaspoon honey
- Salt and black pepper to taste

Directions:

1. Season the salmon fillets with salt and black pepper.
2. Grill the salmon for 4-5 minutes per side or until cooked through.
3. In a large bowl, arrange salad greens and top with diced mango, sliced avocado, thinly sliced red onion, chopped cilantro, and toasted pine nuts.
4. Flake the grilled salmon over the salad.

5. In a small bowl, whisk together orange juice, lime juice, olive oil, honey, salt, and black pepper to make the citrus vinaigrette.
6. Drizzle the salad with the citrus vinaigrette and toss gently to combine.
7. Serve immediately.

Greek Salmon Salad with Tzatziki Dressing

Embark on a journey to Greece with our Greek Salmon Salad featuring Tzatziki Dressing. Grilled salmon, olives, feta cheese, and crisp vegetables are crowned with a refreshing tzatziki dressing. This salad celebrates Mediterranean flavors, offering a taste of the Aegean in every bite.

TOTAL TIME cooking: 25 minutes

Ingredients:

- 1 pound salmon fillets
- Salt and black pepper to taste
- 8 cups mixed salad greens
- 1 cup cherry tomatoes, halved
- 1 cucumber, diced
- 1/2 cup Kalamata olives, sliced
- 1/2 cup feta cheese, crumbled
- Red onion, thinly sliced
- Fresh oregano, chopped, for garnish

Tzatziki Dressing:

- 1 cup Greek yogurt
- 1 cucumber, grated and drained
- 2 cloves garlic, minced
- 2 tablespoons fresh dill, chopped
- 1 tablespoon olive oil
- Salt and black pepper to taste
- Lemon juice to taste

Directions:

1. Season the salmon fillets with salt and black pepper.
2. Grill the salmon for 4-5 minutes per side or until cooked through.

3. In a large bowl, combine salad greens, cherry tomatoes, diced cucumber, sliced Kalamata olives, crumbled feta cheese, red onion, and chopped fresh oregano.
4. Flake the grilled salmon over the salad.
5. In a separate bowl, mix Greek yogurt, grated cucumber, minced garlic, chopped fresh dill, olive oil, salt, black pepper, and lemon juice to make the tzatziki dressing.
6. Drizzle the salad with the tzatziki dressing and toss gently to combine.
7. Serve immediately.

Caprese Salmon Salad

Experience the classic combination of tomatoes, mozzarella, and basil with a salmon twist in our Caprese Salmon Salad. Grilled salmon elevates the traditional Caprese salad, creating a harmonious blend of textures and flavors. Drizzled with balsamic glaze, this salad is a true Italian-inspired delight.

TOTAL TIME cooking: 20 minutes

Ingredients:

- 1 pound salmon fillets
- Salt and black pepper to taste
- 6 cups mixed salad greens
- 1 cup cherry tomatoes, halved
- Fresh mozzarella balls, halved
- Fresh basil leaves
- Balsamic glaze for drizzling

Basil Pesto Vinaigrette:

- 1/4 cup basil pesto
- 2 tablespoons balsamic vinegar
- 3 tablespoons olive oil
- Salt and black pepper to taste

Directions:

1. Season the salmon fillets with salt and black pepper.
2. Grill the salmon for 4-5 minutes per side or until cooked through.
3. Combine salad greens, cherry tomatoes, halved mozzarella balls, and fresh basil leaves in a large bowl.
4. Flake the grilled salmon over the salad.
5. To make the vinaigrette, in a small bowl, mix basil pesto, balsamic vinegar, olive oil, salt, and black pepper.

6. Drizzle the salad with the basil pesto vinaigrette and drizzle the balsamic glaze.
7. Toss gently to combine and serve immediately.

Southwest Salmon Salad with Cilantro Lime Dressing

Spice up your salad game with the Southwest Salmon Salad featuring Cilantro Lime Dressing. The grilled salmon, paired with black beans, corn, and avocado, is complemented by the zesty cilantro lime dressing. This salad is a fusion of bold Southwestern flavors that is satisfying and refreshing.

TOTAL TIME cooking: 30 minutes

Ingredients:

- 1 pound salmon fillets
- 1 tablespoon olive oil
- 1 tablespoon chili powder
- 1 teaspoon cumin
- Salt and black pepper to taste
- 8 cups mixed salad greens
- 1 cup black beans, drained and rinsed
- 1 cup corn kernels (fresh or frozen)
- 1 avocado, sliced
- Cherry tomatoes, halved
- Red onion, thinly sliced
- Fresh cilantro, chopped, for garnish

Cilantro Lime Dressing:

- 1/4 cup fresh lime juice
- 2 tablespoons olive oil
- 2 tablespoons fresh cilantro, chopped
- 1 clove garlic, minced
- Salt and black pepper to taste

Directions:

1. Preheat the oven to 400°F (200°C).
2. Rub salmon fillets with olive oil, chili powder, cumin, salt, and black pepper.
3. Bake the salmon for 15-18 minutes or until cooked.
4. In a large bowl, combine salad greens, black beans, corn, sliced avocado, cherry tomatoes, and thinly sliced red onion.
5. Flake the baked salmon over the salad.
6. In a small bowl, whisk together lime juice, olive oil, chopped cilantro, minced garlic, salt, and black pepper to make the dressing.
7. Drizzle the salad with the cilantro lime dressing and toss gently to combine.
8. Garnish with chopped fresh cilantro and serve immediately.

Teriyaki Glazed Salmon Salad

Delight your taste buds with the Teriyaki Glazed Salmon Salad. The sweet and savory teriyaki-glazed salmon, combined with crisp vegetables and leafy greens, creates a salad that is as visually appealing as it is delicious. The teriyaki glaze adds an Asian-inspired flair, making this dish a perfect balance of flavors.

TOTAL TIME cooking: 25 minutes

Ingredients:

- 1 pound salmon fillets
- 1/4 cup teriyaki sauce
- Salt and black pepper to taste
- 8 cups mixed salad greens
- 1 cup snap peas, trimmed
- 1 carrot, julienned
- 1 red bell pepper, thinly sliced
- 1/2 cup cashews, toasted
- Sesame seeds for garnish

Ginger Soy Vinaigrette:

- 2 tablespoons soy sauce
- 1 tablespoon rice vinegar
- 1 tablespoon sesame oil
- 1 tablespoon honey
- 1 teaspoon fresh ginger, grated
- 1 clove garlic, minced

Directions:

1. Preheat the oven to 400°F (200°C).
2. Brush salmon fillets with teriyaki sauce and bake for 15-18 minutes or until cooked.
3. Season the salmon with salt and black pepper.

4. Combine salad greens, snap peas, julienned carrot, thinly sliced red bell pepper, and toasted cashews in a large bowl.
5. Flake the baked salmon over the salad.
6. In a small bowl, whisk together soy sauce, rice vinegar, sesame oil, honey, grated ginger, and minced garlic to make the vinaigrette.
7. Drizzle the salad with the ginger soy vinaigrette and toss gently to combine.
8. Garnish with sesame seeds and serve immediately.

Raspberry Walnut Salmon Salad

Indulge in a symphony of sweet and savory notes with our Raspberry Walnut Salmon Salad. Grilled salmon, fresh raspberries, and crunchy walnuts come together in this delightful salad. The raspberry vinaigrette adds a burst of fruity goodness, creating an elegant and delicious salad.

TOTAL TIME cooking: 20 minutes

Ingredients:

- 1 pound salmon fillets
- Salt and black pepper to taste
- 6 cups mixed salad greens
- 1 cup fresh raspberries
- 1/2 cup feta cheese, crumbled
- 1/2 cup walnuts, toasted and chopped
- Red onion, thinly sliced
- Balsamic vinaigrette for drizzling

Raspberry Vinaigrette:

- 1/2 cup fresh raspberries
- 2 tablespoons balsamic vinegar
- 1/4 cup olive oil
- 1 tablespoon honey
- Salt and black pepper to taste

Directions:

1. Season the salmon fillets with salt and black pepper.
2. Grill the salmon for 4-5 minutes per side or until cooked through.
3. Combine salad greens, fresh raspberries, crumbled feta cheese, chopped toasted walnuts, and thinly sliced red onion in a large bowl.
4. Flake the grilled salmon over the salad.

5. Combine raspberries, balsamic vinegar, olive oil, honey, salt, and black pepper to make the raspberry vinaigrette in a blender.
6. Drizzle the salad with the raspberry vinaigrette and toss gently to combine.
7. Drizzle balsamic vinaigrette on top and serve immediately.

Classic Salmon Cakes

Delight in the timeless appeal of our Classic Salmon Cakes. These cakes feature flaky salmon bound together with a perfect blend of herbs and breadcrumbs. Pan-fried to golden perfection, they offer a crispy exterior that gives way to a moist and flavorful interior. This classic rendition is a must-try for those who appreciate the simple pleasures of well-executed salmon cakes.

TOTAL TIME COOKING: 30 minutes

Ingredients:

- 1 pound salmon fillets, cooked and flaked
- 1 cup breadcrumbs
- 1/4 cup mayonnaise
- 1/4 cup finely chopped red onion
- 2 tablespoons chopped fresh parsley
- 1 tablespoon Dijon mustard
- 1 teaspoon lemon zest
- 1 egg, beaten
- Salt and black pepper to taste
- Olive oil for frying

Directions:

1. Combine flaked salmon, breadcrumbs, mayonnaise, red onion, parsley, Dijon mustard, lemon zest, beaten egg, salt, and black pepper in a large bowl.
2. Place the mixture into patties on a baking sheet.
3. Heat olive oil in a skillet over medium heat.
4. Cook the salmon cakes for 3-4 minutes per side or until golden brown.
5. Serve hot with your favorite dipping sauce.

Spicy Sriracha Salmon Cakes

Ignite your taste buds with our Spicy Sriracha Salmon Cakes. These bold and fiery cakes feature the perfect marriage of sriracha heat and succulent salmon. Pan-fried to perfection, they offer a spicy kick that adds an exciting twist to the classic salmon cake—a perfect choice for those who crave a bit of heat in their culinary adventures.

TOTAL TIME COOKING: 35 minutes

Ingredients:

- 1 pound canned pink salmon, drained and flaked
- 1/2 cup Panko breadcrumbs
- 1/4 cup mayonnaise
- 2 green onions, finely chopped
- 1 tablespoon sriracha sauce
- 1 teaspoon soy sauce
- 1 teaspoon lime juice
- 1 egg, beaten
- Salt and black pepper to taste
- Vegetable oil for frying

Directions:

1. Combine flaked salmon, Panko breadcrumbs, mayonnaise, chopped green onions, sriracha sauce, soy sauce, lime juice, beaten egg, salt, and black pepper in a mixing bowl.
2. Form the mixture into patties.
3. Heat vegetable oil in a skillet over medium heat.
4. Fry the salmon cakes for 3-4 minutes per side until crispy and golden.
5. Serve with a lime wedge and extra sriracha for those who like it extra spicy.

Lemon Herb Salmon Cakes

Elevate your salmon cakes with the bright flavors of lemon and a medley of fresh herbs, creating a light and refreshing dish.

TOTAL TIME COOKING: 25 minutes

Ingredients:

- 1 pound fresh salmon fillets, cooked and flaked
- 1/2 cup breadcrumbs
- 1/4 cup mayonnaise
- 2 tablespoons chopped fresh dill
- 2 tablespoons chopped fresh chives
- 1 tablespoon lemon juice
- 1 teaspoon lemon zest
- 1 egg, beaten
- Salt and black pepper to taste
- Olive oil for frying

Directions:

1. Mix flaked salmon, breadcrumbs, mayonnaise, fresh dill, chives, lemon juice, lemon zest, beaten egg, salt, and black pepper in a bowl.
2. Shape the mixture into patties.
3. Heat olive oil in a skillet over medium heat.
4. Cook the salmon cakes for 3-4 minutes per side or until golden brown.
5. Serve with a lemon wedge and a dollop of dill-infused mayonnaise.

Mediterranean-Inspired Salmon Cakes

Transport your taste buds to the shores of the Mediterranean with our Mediterranean-inspired salmon Cakes. These cakes feature the flavors of olives, sun-dried tomatoes, and Mediterranean herbs, creating a savory and aromatic experience. Pan-fried to perfection, these cakes offer a taste of the coastal cuisine.

TOTAL TIME COOKING: 40 minutes

Ingredients:

- 1 pound canned red salmon, drained and flaked
- 1/2 cup breadcrumbs
- 1/4 cup crumbled feta cheese
- 1/4 cup chopped Kalamata olives
- 2 tablespoons chopped fresh parsley
- 1 tablespoon lemon juice
- 1 teaspoon dried oregano
- 1 egg, beaten
- Salt and black pepper to taste
- Olive oil for frying

Directions:

1. Combine flaked salmon, breadcrumbs, feta cheese, Kalamata olives, parsley, lemon juice, dried oregano, beaten egg, salt, and black pepper in a bowl.
2. Form the mixture into patties.
3. Heat olive oil in a skillet over medium heat.
4. Fry the salmon cakes for 4-5 minutes per side until they have a golden crust.
5. Serve with a side of tzatziki sauce for a delightful Mediterranean touch.

Asian-Inspired Sesame Salmon Cakes

Infuse an Asian flair with sesame seeds, ginger, and soy sauce into your salmon cakes, creating a savory and satisfying dish.

TOTAL TIME COOKING: 30 minutes

Ingredients:

- 1 pound fresh salmon fillets, cooked and flaked
- 1/2 cup Panko breadcrumbs
- 2 tablespoons soy sauce
- 1 tablespoon sesame oil
- 1 tablespoon chopped green onions
- 1 teaspoon grated ginger
- 1 teaspoon sesame seeds
- 1 egg, beaten
- Salt and black pepper to taste
- Vegetable oil for frying

Directions:

1. Mix flaked salmon, Panko breadcrumbs, soy sauce, sesame oil, chopped green onions, grated ginger, sesame seeds, beaten egg, salt, and black pepper in a bowl.
2. Shape the mixture into patties.
3. Heat vegetable oil in a skillet over medium heat.
4. Cook the salmon cakes for 3-4 minutes per side or until golden and crispy.
5. Serve with a drizzle of extra soy sauce and sprinkle with additional sesame seeds.

Printed in Great Britain
by Amazon

37164603R00050